Stranger on the Plains

A Spiritual Journey

G. Keith Gunderson

Copyright

Copyright © 2025 G. Keith Gunderson
Published by

All rights reserved. No part of this book may be reproduced or transmitted in any form or by any means, electronic or mechanical, including photocopying, recording, or by any information storage and retrieval system, without written permission from the publisher and author.

Dedication

To Noel— my hope

And my horizon.

Foreword

In 1977 I came back to Southwestern North Dakota (just those three words identify a big empty place needing to be filled with meaning) I was a fresh graduate from Wartburg Theological Seminary in Dubuque Iowa where I had lived for four years in ravines, tall trees, and humidity and water along the shores of the great river. I came back to a rural parish on the edge of the Badlands, where Montana, South Dakota and North Dakota meet. I returned with a "call" and the blessing of a Bishop, but I came back because I needed to come back. I did not know why.

In the next few years that "why?" Why did you come back to a place so close to you home was prodded, poked, and partly answered by a mentor. His name was G Keith Gunderson. His background was similar to mine. He was born and grew up near my home, our towns were rivals, and we both attended a small state teachers' college a few years apart.

I registered for a class in something called the Great Plains Institute Of Theology. I participated in a Symposium called the Dakota Mystique. I met lay people, preachers, writers and thinkers with roots in this place. But it was G Keith Gunderson who taught a class called, if I remember rightly called "Dakotah Isaiah". That class was where the book took shape.

And that class shaped my thinking, writing and work from those early years until now. I first heard these stories told and read in that class. Gunderson's unique weave of theology, geography, sociology, metaphor, autobiography, culture and "The Book" shaped the way I would approach my whole life. It made me think and feel in a way that connected music, life on the plains, this universe and what we Lutherans and others call The Word.

I will sum up the book. I will recommend it highly and tell you I am pretty danged excited to hold the copy in my hands and read it, experience, relive and live its themes again.

Reverend Rick Watson

North Dakota Associate Poet Laureate

Table of Contents

PRELUDE	7
PART ONE	8
Chapter 1	9
Chapter 2	10
Chapter 3	12
Chapter 4	13
Chapter 5	15
Chapter 6	16
Chapter 7	18
Chapter 8	19
Chapter 9	20
Chapter 10	21
Chapter 11	23
Chapter 12	24
Chapter 13	25
Chapter 14	26
Chapter 15	27
Chapter 16	28
Chapter 17	29
PART TWO	32
Chapter 18	33
Chapter 19	34
Chapter 20	35
Chapter 21	36
Chapter 22	38
Chapter 23	39
Chapter 24	40
Chapter 25	41
Chapter 26	42
Chapter 27	43
Chapter 28	44
Chapter 29	45
Chapter 30	47
Chapter 31	48
Chapter 32	49
Chapter 33	50
Chapter 34	51
Chapter 35	52
Chapter 36	53
Chapter 37	54
Chapter 38	55
Chapter 39	56

Chapter 40 57
Chapter 41 58
Chapter 42 59
Chapter 43 60
Chapter 44 61
Chapter 45 62
Chapter 46 64
Chapter 47 65
PART THREE 67
Chapter 48 68
Chapter 49 69
Chapter 50 71
Chapter 51 72
Chapter 52 73
Chapter 53 74
Chapter 54 75
Chapter 55 76
Chapter 56 77
Chapter 57 78
Chapter 58 80
Chapter 59 81
Chapter 60 82
Chapter 61 83
Chapter 62 86
Chapter 63 87
Chapter 64 89
Chapter 65 90
Postlude 91

PRELUDE

"So the Gunderson's got a preacher," he said.

He sat on the edge of his white hospital bed, a leathered form in faded blue pajamas, his ulcered foot inflamed and bandaged, and puffed a Camel. His words altered time and transformed the room.

"It's too bad 'Mother' isn't here for this," they were saying, aunts and uncles gathered in my parents' backyard after my ordination into the ministry that morning. We had gathered for her, 'Mother', my granmother, about a dozen years earlier up in Miles City.

Years later I received her Birthday Book, in Norwegian, Bible verses and pieces of old hymns; dates and names of every Gunderson I ever knew and some strangers. My date was there. It was a small, yellow-green book, faded, cloth worn away at the corners, pages yellow and loose. Inside the cover, scrawled in the familiar hand I had seen on birthday cards many times, an inscription read: "This is a memento by my granmother presented to her grandaughter Mathilde unto the fifth generation at this writing the memorial year of 1919 'Dad died' written by Mother."It was the longest entry in the book.

Further on, on the blank page opposite the Bible verse and hymn piece for January 7, in s o f t purple ink, it was written: "Gerhard H. Gunderson, fodt, tune Prestigfeld Greager den 7 Januar 1872 Norge." Below, scribbled broadly in black, "Died den 18 August i 1919 in Harding County So. Dak." The word "died" was misspelled, corrected over in pencil by a later hand.

He crumpled out his Camel in the black plastic ashtray, gray ash, crumpled white cylinder, brushed his yellowed fingers off, and lit another one up. The sulphur brought back time and the room.I looked into his rugged face.

"Yeah, I guess they did," I said. He seemed satisfied with that. He went on chain-smoking Camels and kept his conversation close to the ground. He was a thin man with a long face, leathered by forty years of battling bachelorhood and the sun. He spoke abruptly, as one not accustomed to conversation.

They gathered for him a couple of weeks later at the Funeral Home in Bowman. After the service they hauled him out to a cemetery by a deserted church near Ludlow, South Dakota. They laid the casket on the ground before the grave, piles of dirt on either side of the pit. I thought I smelled leather and Camel cigarettes as I stood there and some preacher named Gunderson read the committal to the wind and the huddled family few and friends.

"Let's go grab some lunch," one of the pallbearers said after it was over. "We'll come back and throw some dirt on him later." And we went up to his sister's, a half mile east, up on the bluff, for coffee and conversation.

PART ONE

Psalm before sunrise

Last Monday morning at 5 a.m.

I woke up to the sound of music.

A million pre-dawn birds were singing up the sun in the east.

It made Beethoven's beautiful Fifth sound as

artless as the latest Johnny Paycheck.

Last Monday morning at 5 a.m.

I woke up to the sound of music.

A million pre-dawn birds were singing up the sun in the east.

Stravinsky never sounded better. Hallelujah.

Chapter 1

Monday morning, Jerusalem. The sun had drifted over India and Kubla Khan by now, but it hadn't yet risen here. By mid-day, the gold-faced buildings would shine, as would the golden rings on the fingers of Passover pilgrims, the golden bracelets on their arms, the golden earrings in their ears, and the golden necklaces around their necks. But for now, the city remained in shadow. There was a stirring, though, in the pre-dawn darkness of the market streets, as merchants polished their wares and prepared to set them out for another day. In the distance, on the edge of dawn, the outlines of camel caravans belonging to foreign traders began to form. These traders would arrive in the city and set up in the market streets by noon.

The pre-dawn birds sang up the sun, but the winepresses were silent. They had been working overtime, and the wine cellars were full. The stonecutters rose, the carpenters awakened, and the money changers in the temple began to count out their money. Beggars hurried to their stations in the streets. The priests in the temple sharpened their knives for the slaughter of the sacrificial animals—a ritual that would continue all day and far into the night, every night, all week. The blood would eventually drip down off the platform, down the steps, out onto the ground, and down the slopes of Zion.

Monday morning, Jerusalem. On a hill outside the city, a man awakened and rose. His friends dozed on, exhausted from their trip into the city the day before. They had returned outside last night, unable to find room anywhere within the city walls.

Chapter 2

"I never knew my grandpa," I said. We were sitting on Shelf Rock, overlooking the old golf course northeast of Hettinger. A rooster pheasant strutted across the seventh green, its feathers a vibrant splash against the sand. "He died of pneumonia in 1919," I continued. "I wasn't born until '43. I did see a picture of him once, though—bearded the summer before his death. That beard hid his face from me for many years. But one night last October, my father shaved off that beard for a moment and let me see. There was uncommon emotion in my father's face and voice and eyes the night he told me the story of Grandpa's windmill." I paused to watch the pheasant. Low cumulus clouds were banking dark in the northwest, their undersides lit by the fading sun.

"Grandpa brought his family out here from Iowa in 1910 to America's Last Frontier, Harding County, South Dakota. He settled down on a hundred and sixty acres of what used to be called The Great American Desert. And he quickly learned, as men who came out here did, that water was scarce, and that it had to be brought up from veins beneath the prairie." I paused again. The clouds were coming together, casting a dark, dark blue shadow beneath them.

"He drilled a well in the far corner of his homestead quarter and went to work to build himself a windmill. He had neither the proper tools nor the right parts, so he took an old binder reel, nailed wide boards onto the slats, fastened it atop his first homestead shack, and moved the shack over by the well. Onto the homemade windmill, he hooked a homemade shaft—a pitman from an old mower—and connected it to the pump." I tried to draw a picture for him in the air with my hands as I talked. The northwestern sky was getting darker, and closer.

"But it didn't have a governor," I continued. "And the Harding County wind spun the ungoverned reel wildly, causing the homemade shaft to move up and down much, much too quickly. It broke almost every time the windmill spun." He smiled, a hint of amusement in his eyes.

"Grandpa spent countless precious homestead hours tinkering with and repairing his windmill. He still didn't have it right when he contracted the flu during the great epidemic of '18." Thunder rumbled in the distance, a low growl that seemed to shake the air.

Grandpa never fully recovered from the windmills or the flu. My father remembers him sitting silently in his chair by the window that next summer, thinking perhaps about windmills and death. He had a hard time breathing and couldn't work much anymore. He was 47, and he seemed to know that he was soon going to die." Lightning broke through the blue clouds, followed by thunder that boomed and rolled across the landscape.

"'Buy a windmill,' is the last thing my father can remember him telling his mother, my grandmother, before pneumonia came, took his breath away, and the neighbors came over to trim his hair and shave his beard for the last time."

The smell of rain arrived, fresh and cool, as the sun dipped below the horizon, leaving only a golden rim on the top of the front clouds.

"She did buy a windmill after they laid him out. And she stayed on the farm, finishing raising up the ten kids until the well went dry in '32 or '33, and she moved on up into Miles City, Montana." He sat in silence, his eyes beyond me, lost in thought. The wind started up, and the thunder came closer, lightning flashes illuminating the darkening sky. But he didn't move; he didn't seem concerned about it all. I arose and climbed down below the shelf to try to find shelter in one of the caves.

"You coming?" I called up as the rain began to beat against the rocks. But he didn't answer. And he never did come.

Chapter 3

He rubs his eyes, brushes back his hair, and strokes his beard. Beneath him, the golden city lies silent.

In the distance, the lowing of fat cattle destined for the marketplace echoes through the air, mingling with the crowing of roosters and the clucking of plump hens. The faint cries of little lambs, the bleating of sheep, and the cooing of turtledoves fill the morning air—all will be on sale in the city today, victims for the sacrificial feast.

He is silent, taking in the scents of the morning. The aroma of fresh olives fills his nostrils and settles in his memory, accompanied by the faint smell of olive oil. The air is also rich with the fragrance of roses and honey, dates, grapes, and figs.

Dew still clings to the grass, and the air is laden with the sounds and quiet morning fragrances of Passover. He takes a deep breath, letting the morning fill him—olives and roses, visions of beggars hurrying to their stations in the streets, and the symphony of the pre-dawn birds. The eastern sky is painted with hues of yellow, gold, violet, red, and pink, with the shadow of the moon hanging high above.

He takes another deep breath. The scent of cinnamon wafts through the air, signaling that the priests must be awake, too. As a breeze stirs, the scent of cinnamon incense from the temple rises out of the valley and into his nostrils—a pleasant smell that complements the morning's tranquility. It is a pleasant morning. He is full of life and praise.

Chapter 4

The storm had passed. I climbed out of the cave and wondered where he was. The seventh green looked like a swimming pool, and the pheasant was gone. I climbed back up onto the wet shelf. He was sitting where I had left him, seemingly untouched by the rain. I narrowed my eyes.

"Are you ready to go?" I asked.

He arose and brushed himself off. I was hesitant to ask what he had done during the storm. We started down the rock. A dog in the yard of a house over on the southern bluff barked. We walked on.

"I used to have a dog named after a president," I said. "He was an exquisite red cocker spaniel with large, wet cocker spaniel eyes and long, soft, silky cocker spaniel ears." I glanced over to see if he was listening.

"Which president?" he asked without looking my way or breaking stride.

"His name was Ike," I replied. "I bought him from my third-grade teacher for $5 when she and her husband moved away to California and couldn't take him along."

As we started up the last hill into town, a flickertail watched us from the wet grass. It darted away as we approached.

"He was by far the finest dog I ever had," I continued. "When the weather was nice, I would sit on the step and scratch him behind the ears. Sometimes we would roll around on the ground and play. Inside the house at night, he would sit beside me or lie down at my feet. During mealtime, he would stand up on his haunches and beg mercilessly, staring out with those big cocker spaniel eyes at whomever might feed him." I mimicked his begging posture, bringing my hands up to my chest, drooping my wrists, and sticking out my tongue to pant. It looked like he smiled.

"Sometimes he slept in my bed. He went wherever I went, except to school. And during the summer, he would trot alongside my bike on the way to and from Baseball practice."

The dog on the bluff had stopped barking. Meadowlarks sang on the fence, and a vehicle we couldn't see rolled by on the street just over the hill.

"But one summer he started to change," I said. "When I stepped outside to call him in, he didn't come. He began to be gone for a few hours at a time, sometimes not even returning at night."

As we crested the hill, the roofs of the houses on the edge of town came into view.

"On the way to and from baseball practice, he began to wander farther and farther away from my bike. My parents started to worry about his running around," I said as we stepped off the grass onto the gravel of the first street. "They said it was no good to have a dog like that." He remained silent. Children laughed in the yard of the green house with the brown roof. A woman, wearing a wide-brimmed straw bonnet to shade out the sun, was on her knees, digging among her flowers.

"I tried to keep him close to me when I went around town and made him stay at home to prevent him from running around. But it didn't work. Almost every time someone opened the door, he slipped out and was gone off to wherever it was he went. I began to hear rumors that he was running around town with a pack of other dogs."

We started down the hill to the street that curved around the edge of town. "I had to work harder to keep him beside me on my way to and from baseball practice. I even used a leash sometimes."

As we circled the north edge of town, I remembered the time I came home from there with a fistful of crocuses for my mother from beyond the barb wire fence..

"But one day as I rode up over the tracks at the south end of Main Street and up to the theater by the corner, turning west, Ike didn't turn. He took off up the street. I called and called, but he didn't come back. Our relationship changed after that. I knew I couldn't keep him anymore."

We turned south at Dr. Schumacher's and started down Main Street. I wondered if the crabapples in the backyard across the street were ripe. The sidewalks were already dry.

"That fall, I sold him to another teacher of mine who lived out at the Agricultural Experiment Station on the west edge of town. She paid me $10."

Chapter 5

He walks silently away from his sleeping friends, stepping carefully so that he does not disturb them. The Passover story begins to form in him—Moses, Pharaoh, the Hebrews: Bricks, plagues, the slaughter of the firstborn, the Spirit passing over the homes of those with blood marked door posts.

And now, beyond the hearing of his friends, he turns his face towards the east, stretches out his arms, and prays:

"Your love, O Lord,

reaches to the heavens,

and your faithfulness to the clouds."

Psalm 36, It is as if it had been composed out of his own depths. He knows it by heart.

"Your righteousness is like the strong mountains.

Your justice is like the great deep;

You save man and beast, O Lord."

As he speaks, memories of his friends come to him, and the forms of the men and women in the city below. He remembers all the pilgrims who, like him, are scattered in the surrounding hills.

And the little children, how they come and climb onto his lap and sit while he talking, and stroke his cheeks and beard.

The clucking hens, the crowing roosters, the lowing cattle, the pre-dawn birds, the donkey he rode into town on yesterday —the lambs, the doves, the sheep, the calves, bleating, cooing, bawling—all the sacrificial beasts pass through too.

"How priceless is your love, O God: Your people take refuge

under the shadow of your wings.

They feast upon the abundance of your house; you give them drink

from the river of your thoughts.

The faint scent of cinnamon and roses come back to him again. He pauses and takes a deep breath.

"For with you is the well of life, and in your light we see light.

Continue your loving kindness to those who know you,

and your favor to those who are true of heart."

Chapter 6

We pulled up at the street corner to wait for the cars to pass.

"The teacher I sold him to lived just down the road and up from us a ways," I said. "But I never went to see Ike there. My parents said I shouldn't, because then he'd want to run away and come home with me."

"But the next winter, I heard that he was running around anyway." I jumped over the puddle left at the curb by a dam of debris. "The next spring, they moved away, and I heard they gave him to a farmer out east of town. And I forgot about him."

Up the street, men in the raised bucket of a utilities repair truck were repairing wires broken by a tree that had fallen during the storm. Other men stood below, throwing twigs and branches onto another truck.

"A few years later, I saw him again, though," I continued. "It was in the alley across the street from the Post Office. He was as handsome as ever; his red coat shone in the autumn afternoon sun. But some of the sparkle had gone from his eyes, and he cowered slightly. I guessed that his new master, whoever he was, must have tried to beat the wanderlust out of him."

"But he had run away, maybe for good this time. We stood across the alley from each other." I stopped to act out the scene. "Ike," I called, "Come here, Eisenhower, old boy." His eyes lit up for a moment, and he wagged his tail once. But he didn't come.

"Come here, Ike," I called again, stepping toward him, expecting him to come and jump up on me and lick my face like he used to. He just cowered a little and backed away. I crouched down, held out my hand, and called to him again, but the light of recognition had disappeared from his eyes, and he stood his ground.

"He didn't seem to know me anymore," I said, getting up, straightening out my jeans, and beginning to walk again. "He was no longer my dog. He had made a life out of running. He belonged to someone else and to someone else again. He ran around during the day and he ran around at night."

"He passed from owner to owner, from master to master, until he couldn't recognize the voice of the one who loved him anymore. He stood his ground for a few moments and looked at me. Each time I edged closer, he backed farther away.

"He turned and disappeared down the alley and through someone's yard. I never saw him again."

We walked on in silence. After we had passed the line-repair truck and the voices of the men were small, he spoke.

"I had a dog like that once," he said.

"Really?" I replied.

"What was his name?"

"Her name," he corrected.

"Her name," I said.

"Jerusalem," he answered.

Chapter 7

The sun is up now. The morning stars have faded, the birds are silent, and the sky is clearing in the east. Down below in other valleys, he can make out fields of corn, grain, and pulse. Some of the golden buildings are beginning to brighten, and he can smell the scent of honey coming from somewhere. And cinnamon.

He hears footsteps behind him, followed by silence. A small voice calls. He recognizes the voice. He turns. "What is it, John?" he asks.

"I woke up and couldn't find you," John explains, "and I wondered where you were."

"I'm right here, John, right here," he reassures him. He steps toward his worried friend and puts his arm around his shoulder. They turn back towards camp.

"Can you smell the cinnamon, John?" he asks as they begin to walk back to their friends.

Chapter 8

Night fell, bringing stars with it. The rain had washed the buildings clean. Far up Main Street, a neon light blinked its pink message: "Mecca Bar." Down the street, across the tracks, beyond the park, we crouched on the shore of Mirror Lake and tossed pebbles into its darkness.

The gentle plip of the pebbles broke the silence. Lights from across the way reflected on the surface. "I remember a ride, alone in the back of my uncle's pickup on a late summer night across an almost endless South Dakota prairie," I said.

He looked at me, turned, and threw another pebble into the darkness. "We had been to visit a sheepherder—my dad, my uncle, and I. As I sat outside on the step of the sheepwagon, playing with the dog, I heard them talk about the day's rumors of hail and speculate about damage to the unharvested grain. They laughed and drank and played cards together until someone began to pull the curtain of night over the quiet prairie."

"So we were on our way back home. I lay in the back of the bumpy pickup, alone, gazing up at the million bright stars above me. It had rained earlier in the day, but the clouds had now all passed over, leaving only the fresh memory and the smell of wet sagebrush for us travelers of the night. As I lay there drinking in the silent beauty of the stars, I was suddenly very frightened. I felt so small, so sad, so alone in the huge universe. I began to imagine lights moving across the heavens—flying saucers, I thought. It was the Fifties; they were popular then. Was there life somewhere out there, perhaps other boys like me riding in the back of a pickup into the darkness across a wide prairie on another planet, somewhere?

"Crickets chirped, and far away dogs barked. And a coyote howled at the moon." The ten o'clock whistle broke the silence. The moon had risen bigger than life in the east. He was looking at it. We both watched until it shrunk down to size and started to sail small across the August heavens.

Chapter 9

Tuesday morning. It is about the fourth hour. The streets are beginning to fill with people and noise. He and his friends have already eaten breakfast—figs, olives, a piece of lamb, the breast of a turtledove, and goat's milk—and oiled down their beards and hair. They have come down from the hill, descending into the city, which is coming alive with the activities of Passover.

Roman soldiers are stationed here and there along the streets, ready to draw their swords if things start to get out of hand. The scent of cinnamon has given way to the smells of sweat, manure, bread, and fruit—flour, olive oil, and grain.

The sounds of cattle, chickens, turtledoves, and sheep mingle with the voices of the sellers and the arguments of the buyers. Beggars, blind, crippled, leprous, and deaf, reach out with bony fingers. Officials strut and preen in their palaces and on palace lawns. Priests and patriots hurry from building to building.

Children run unattended everywhere as traders unpack their camels and begin to sell their wares.

Chapter 10

Riding the backroads across the morning prairie, we came upon two mounted riders. They hailed us, and we hailed back. They disappeared in the dust and gravel.

"I worked for a rancher near here one summer," I said, "topping haystacks for him by spreading the hay the bucket delivered up to me evenly across the top of the stack." He looked out beyond the windbreak, where men were working in the field. Cows huddled in the corner of the pasture, swishing flies with their tails.

"It was hard work in the hot sun, but it was cut short for a few days by rain. It would rain off and on during the day, drizzle and mist a little in between, and fog in the morning. So my boss decided we should go out and move the cows.

"I was given a big bay to ride, an elegant-looking dark reddish-brown animal with a black mane and tail." He leaned back and closed his eyes.

"The boss told me it was a rough horse, but the most predictable one he had. He was looking out for me, knowing I hadn't been on a horse for over two years, and before that not much. I used to ride Frosty, a 20-year-old buckskin, out to get the milk cows every day one summer for my Harding County uncle, but that was about all.

A picture came to mind of a boy in the saddle of the blunt, brown animal, riding out through the corral, past the watertower, down the alley between the corral and the garden, and out into the pasture. Sometimes he stood up on the saddle and let the reins go, looking for the cows.

"I put my booted foot into the stirrup and climbed up into the saddle like a real cowboy.

"The horse was rough, but predictable. We rode across the wet prairie and in and out of draws and over hills most of the morning.

I glanced over. His head was still back, his eyes closed. He didn't move. 'When we finished, we headed back to the place,' I said, turning back to the windshield. 'I was told to go on alone. The boss and the others had a couple of other things to do.' So I rode on until the barn of the place became bigger, and I could see each board and the trees took on their individual shapes and colors. I was tired and wet. I began to feel every uneven step of the horse.

"A little ways from home, I pulled up beside the stream, slid down off the saddle, and stretched and moved around while the horse drank. It was hard to walk. My body was sore from mid-back down. It was only another half-mile home, though, so I reached for the reins.

"The horse pulled back and trotted a few steps away. Then he stopped and turned and looked at me like a naughty child.

"I moved my aching body step by painful step toward him, but as soon as I got close enough to reach out for the reins again, he turned and trotted a few more steps.

"It started to rain. The place began to look like it was a mile and a half away instead of only half a mile. My body started to feel worse. I was tired and sore and very angry. My legs protested every step.

"The horse turned and galloped back to the place, alone, with its proud head high. He turned in at the fence and disappeared among the buildings.

"After I got home, and after the others had returned, I told them what had happened.

'That horse always does that,' my boss said. 'Sorry I forgot to tell you.'

I looked over again. He was still leaning back, eyes closed. His mouth looked like it was turned up at the corners. I couldn't tell whether he had been listening or whether he was asleep, dreaming pleasant dreams. We drove on.

***

The air seems heavier than it did yesterday or the day before. His friends are at his elbows, pointing here and there, and chattering with the crowd that is beginning to trail along and call out his name.

He would like to go off somewhere by himself. But he is trapped by the heavy air, by the closeness of his friends, and by the crowd.

He begins to pray silently…"In you, O Lord, I have taken refuge,

Let me never be ashamed In your righteousness deliver me and set me free,

incline your ear to me and save me."

Chapter 11

"So, he forgot to tell you?" he said. We were standing atop a high butte, with rocks jutting out in small shelves. "I didn't know you were listening," I replied.

Sweet clover in bloom filled the morning air with its yellow fragrance. He gazed out at the distant hills. "Sometimes I feel like I'm being absorbed into the land," he said, widening his stance and stretching out his arms as he spoke to the distant hills. "My arms and legs turn into prairie roads and highways. People drive their cars, pickups, motorcycles, buses, and trucks upon my limbs. And my chest and stomach turn into the prairie itself."

He relaxed and began to sway with the rhythm of his words.

"Tractors pulling disks and drills carve my belly into a vast checkerboard of wheat and summer fallow. Cattle graze at my chest. Men sink wells into my skin and erect windmills to draw water up from my veins. Prairie dogs burrow in my nose and mouth, coyotes camp out in my ears."

"My fingers and toes sink into the soil and become roots. My hair turns into the long grasses, blowing up and down the sides of steep ditches in spring and summer. My eyes are twin prairie sloughs staring up at the open sky of day and the wide prairie night, up at the lightning, hail, rain, and snow."

"The wind blows and blows across my face and body. Sparrows, hawks, ducks, meadowlarks, and robins fly above. Pheasants nest upon me, and jackrabbits race over me. My flesh is familiar with the hoof of the bison and the pronghorn antelope."

"Sometimes I feel like I'm being absorbed into the land, into the dust from which I was taken. Sometimes I feel like I truly belong to this world, to this time and this place, to this body doomed to death. And that is how it ought to be. For if I didn't belong to this world, to this time and this place, to the land, I would be of no use to God (who loves it, too) or to all my brothers and sisters who are living out their lives here with me."

"I belong to the land, and I will not fade until Death or Something comes along and tears me out by the roots and tries to plant me somewhere else."

He stood looking out across the prairie, a herd of antelope grazing near some distant wheat. He kept his arms stretched out like a scarecrow and stood like that for what seemed a long, long while, his eyes lost in the blue hills. Then his breathing became mournfully heavy, like that of a cancer patient near the end. I wanted to go and try to comfort him, but I was frozen. It seemed like a chasm— deeper than any I would ever want to fall into and wider than I could ever cross— had opened up between us.

Chapter 12

Yesterday morning returns to his memory—the sunrise, the birds, the cinnamon, John—how full of life and praise he was then. The psalm begins to sing within him:

"Be my strong rock,

A castle to keep me safe.

You are my crag and my stronghold.

Deliver me, my God, from the clutches of the evil doer and the oppressor.

"For you are my hope, O Lord, God, my confidence since I was young.

I have been sustained by you ever since I was born:

From my mother's womb you have been my strength; my praise shall be always of you."

A distant voice brings back the sounds of the crowded street. The Psalm stops.

Chapter 13

As we walked back to the car, a black and white she-mongrel strolled by, followed by three fat pups that trundled behind her, nipping at each other, yipping, and stumbling in play. We stopped to watch.

"I had a pup like that once," I said, moving on. The yips grew smaller as we walked away.

"We found it stray outside our house one day, my brother, my sister, and I, when we lived in Bowman in that house out beyond the northwestern edge of town. But we had another dog, an older family dog, a white and brown rat terrier named Freckles." I glanced over at him.

"Mom and Dad informed us before too long that we just couldn't afford to have two dogs around. So my father did what he had to do. He took a piece of rope, his single-shot .22, a few shells, the pup, and us out to the dumpground one day. We took turns holding the pup in the back seat on the way.

"When we got there, he took out the pup and the rope, tied one end of the rope around the pup's neck and the other end to the bumper of a wreck. Then he let each of us pet it. "Then he told us to stand back. He already had the rifle in his hand. He backed up, pulled back the bolt, slipped in the cartridge, closed the bolt,—the same motion and the same gun I would use to put our aged Freckles out of her misery a dozen or so years later. He pulled back the firing pin and raised the rifle."

"The pup yipped, confused. It jumped out and stretched toward us on the rope, tumbling over, fear and play both written in its dark little eyes. "We called its name, and it sat up and cocked its ears. My father pulled the trigger. It squealed once and rolled over.

"My father ejected the empty cartridge and propped the rifle up against the front fender. He walked up, removed the rope, and brought it back to the car. He picked up the rifle, and we all got back in the car and started home".

Fat black hogs were snouting in the garbage here and there.

The she-mongrel and her pups were out of sight now. We were at the car doors. We opened them and got in. I started up, shifted, and pulled away. I narrowed my eyes,

… thinking of the mongrel and her pups as we drove along."

"Maybe we're all like that," he said.

"Like what?" I asked.

"Like victims," he replied.

Chapter 14

He turns and looks toward the voice. Andrew. "What is it, Andrew?"

Andrew runs, half pulling, half dragging a thin, ragged, wasted figure. "This beggar keeps following us and crying out your name, and he won't leave us alone."

"What do you want, friend?" He asks.

The bony figure beams, falls upon his face at his sandals, weeps, and grabs them. "My sight!" he cries, along with other desperate words about mercy and the Son of David.

"Get up," he orders..

The beggar rises. He wets his fingers on his lips and reaches out to touch the man's eyes. "Be opened," he says.

The beggar opens his mouth and eyes wide, feeling his face in disbelief. "Go to the priest and be purified," he says to him.

But he doesn't listen. He runs off down the street shouting to everyone he meets that he can see.

Chapter 15

Smoke from forest fires burning out of control up in Canada hazed the horizon. The sun parted the heavens, and heat began to rise like snakes from the hood of the car. The back of my shirt dampened.

I looked over. He was still leaning back, eyes closed. "Many winters ago in Bowman," I started, "back before Highway 12 was paved, out behind that old gray house beyond the northwest corner of town, my brother raised rabbits."

The only sounds were the whisper of the tires against the gravel and the ripple of rocks beating in the fender wells.

"He built a neat rabbit house surrounded by a neat chicken wire pen," I continued. "He was going to try to make a little money in those days when a little money wasn't easy to come by. They were such pretty things, his rabbits—all soft and white with shiny deep pink eyes and twitching whiskers."

"He cared for them and fed them with lettuce and other greens thrown out by local cafes and grocery stores. But one morning, when he went out to feed them, the door of the pen was swinging open. Dead rabbits were scattered all around on the bloody snow.

"Someone had broken in during the night and beaten every last one of them to death with a board," I said. "My brother was crying. I was scared. I had never seen him cry like that before. And I was haunted by the rabbits in the red snow."

I pulled over to let a tractor pulling a flatbed of bales pass by. The driver's face was shaded by the brim of his hat. The boys on top waved to us, giggling and pointing until they shrunk and disappeared in the dust.

"Victims," he said as I pulled back onto the road.

I wasn't sure what he meant, but I was afraid to ask. I didn't want to sound like a fool. So I just nodded my head knowingly and pretended to understand.

Chapter 16

He turns and continues walking.

The Psalm returns, rising above the clatter and the cries.

"Let my mouth be full of your praise,

and your glory all the day long.

Do not cast me off in my old age;

Forsake me not when my strength fails."

Chapter 17

"Have mercy on me, O God, according to your lovingkindness," he intoned softly as the trees of Hettinger came into view. "In your great compassion blot out my offenses."

"Out in the entry after the ballgame the other night," I interrupted, "a man called me aside. I've got something for you, he said, moving back out of the stream of people and motioning me to come along. He reached inside his jacket, to his shirt pocket.

"He brought out a yellowed newspaper clipping, opened it up, and pointed to the third person kneeling in the front row of a picture of a former Hettinger Junior Legion baseball team. 'Do you know this guy?' he asked.

"I looked. A familiar face stared back at me—cap brim carefully folded, crown properly creased, the black plastic glasses with silver bows, the cuffed sleeves, the thin arms, the smile... I had seen him many times before, indeed. In a mirror.

"As I looked at it, I started to feel funny inside, and it felt like I was going to blush. So I thanked him and took the clipping home.

"At home, I unfolded it and read the story that went with it. August 12, 1959."

"Wash me through and through from my wickedness and cleanse me from my sin," he whispered.

"The front-page headline said, 'Hettinger Junior Legion Will Compete in State Tournament.' I couldn't remember the person standing behind me in the back row. I looked below the picture and read the names.

"Front row, left to right: Lynn Melling and Len Bortke, bat boys. Elton Davidson (He pitched sometimes and married Claudia Goodspeed. He wrecked his new red Oldsmobile F-85 out east of town one night and splintered his right forearm protecting her face. He couldn't pitch much after that.)"

"For I know my transgressions, and my sin is ever before me..."

"Keith Gunderson (Baseball meant more to the centerfielder than God or anything else in those days.)"

"Against you only have I sinned, and done what is evil in your sight."

"Dennis Johnson (Quiet left-handed first baseman and pitcher from Reeder. I didn't know him very well.); Gary Melling (His fastball looked like a balloon, but his other junk made hitters talk to themselves.); Wayne Walch (he had wrists like posts.) and little Lance Rodman, the jacket boy."

I slowed to check the railroad tracks as we crossed the bridge over the creek that feeds into Mirror Lake.

"And so you are justified when you speak and upright in your judgment..."

"Back row, left to right: Gary Donner (He used to come over from Reeder with Dennis Johnson.); Rick Clement (A mountain of a man. They could hit the ball by him at third, but nobody ever hit one through him.)"

"Indeed I have been wicked from my birth, a sinner from my mother's womb..."

John Samuelson (Tony Fugelsten's nephew. He was from California. He had a nice glove. I used it once. I dropped the first fly that was hit to me with it.); Al Bortke (The coach. He didn't know how to swing a bat himself, but he had the gift of teaching others how to do it right.)"

"For behold, you look for truth deep within me and will make me understand wisdom secretly..."

"Bill Mattis (Slender, but oh, so strong. He flicked the bat up in New Salem and hit a ball over those trees out in left field.); Ed Sahlstrom (He was a better actor.); and Rod Reinke (I saw him from afar at his father's funeral over in Hettinger last year. His father was the high school principal and chemistry teacher.)

"Purge me from my sin and I shall be pure; wash me and I shall be clean indeed."

"The Hettinger Junior Legion baseball team won the regional title by defeating Mandan Training School 19-4 in a game played at Mandan on Sunday. August 9. The local team scored their 19 runs on 11 hits. Wayne Walch proved to be the big hitter for the local team as he went four for four, getting three doubles and a single while driving in seven big runs for the Hettinger team. Gary Melling started the game and went the route to gain credit for the victory.

"Hide your face from my sins and blot out my iniquities."

"The Hettinger team will now enter the Class B State Tournament at New Rockford to be held August 14-16. The local team will play the opening game of the tournament, according to information received by Coach Al Bortke; they will play Oakes.

"Create in me a clean heart, O God, and renew a right spirit within me..."

"The boys appearing in the lineup for the local team last Sunday were Melling, Reinke, Clement, Mattis, Walch, Donner, Gunderson, Johnson, Davidson, Sahlstrom, and Samuelson.

"Cast me not away from your presence and take not your Holy Spirit from me."

We headed east out of Hettinger. Cars were scattered on the parking lots of the hospital and the nursing home. The cemetery was up around the curve. "The next night," I said, recovering my train of thought, "the centerfielder stood above the silent left-handed first baseman and pitcher, kneeling at a different altar, and laid his hands upon his head and said, 'In obedience to the command of our Lord Jesus Christ, I forgive you all your sins.'"

"You should have been there," I added.

"I was," he said as the cemetery evergreens appeared and gray tombstones rose up out of the grass.

PART TWO

O God,

You who divided the

darkness

and the light

Into day and night;

Drive away the dogs of darkness.

who chase us down strange,

unlighted alleys,

and let the familiar animals

of Peace and Love

walk always at our sides.

Chapter 18

"For my enemies are talking against me, and those who lie in wait for my life take counsel together. They say, 'God has forsaken him; go after him and seize him, for there is none to save.'"

The bawling of calves, the bleating of sheep, and the cooing of turtledoves bring him back up out of his prayer. He is passing the temple, alone now, as his friends have gone off to mingle with the crowds. They are excited by the splendor of the city, and the vigor of its marketplace. He can see them looking here and there, pointing at this and that, like rural children.

Soldiers stand beside each building, their plumed helmets and bronze armor reflecting the sun. Along another street, he sees armored officers on their white horses ride by.

He looks down at his own simple garment, at his dusty, sandaled feet. The sun rises toward the middle of the heavens, and the morning dew has evaporated. He can feel perspiration forming on his temples and on his brow, along the hairline.

He walks on. A familiar scent comes to him with the breeze that quickly cools his brow. He pauses, turns toward the temple, and breathes deeply in. But the breeze has died, and his brow quickly warms again. The scent of cinnamon has gone back inside the temple walls.

A small, familiar voice interrupts, far away the first time, nearer the second. It is John again.

He turns to the voice. Out of the crowd, John hurries toward him with one arm out. The psalm comes back to him as he waits:

They say, "God has forsaken him; go after him and seize him, for there is none to save."

Chapter 19

Mourners huddled in a green canvas tent among the trees and the tombstones. The coffin was suspended on a rack above the grave. The hearse, black, long, was at the head of the parked procession of shiny cars. A preacher stood and read.

"Miles City, Montana," I began. "April, 1961." The cemetery slid by the window. "I was sitting with my uncle in his car outside the funeral home. It was raining. We were listening to the heavyweight championship fight on the scratchy car radio...Patterson-Johanneson...and my uncle was speculating on whether the "Swede" or the "_" was going to win.

"Inside the funeral home, beyond the radio and the rain, my parents and other relatives gathered in grief around the casket of my 77-year-old prairie grandmother.

"I had stayed with her in her little white house in Miles City one summer a few years earlier, the time I skinned my toes on the pavement when my bare foot slipped off the broken pedal of the bike I was riding...I got blood poisoning...red streaks shot halfway up my leg. I laid on her hide-a-bed in her living room while she nursed me, changing the hot towels on my leg and bringing an occasional pail of steaming salt water for me to soak my foot in, doctor's orders the heat and the salt were supposed to be able to draw the poison out.

"The next day at the funeral the pastor would read, 'Bless the Lord, O' my soul, and all that is within me bless his holy name 'her favorite psalm.

"But that night, the rain rolled down the windshield in little rivulets, punctuated by the bells between the rounds, as we sat in silence and smoked cigarettes while the 'Swede' and the "_____" slugged it out."

"I can't remember who won," I said.
"The"_____", I think," he replied.
"How do you know?" I asked.

"I was there," he said.

"You were where?" I pressed.

"In the backseat," he answered,

Chapter 20

He sits upon a rock, leaning back against the pomegranate tree. His eyes are closed. The sun is dipping behind the western clouds. It is Wednesday. Judas has changed. His body stays beside him, but his spirit is not there.

"Be pleased, O God, to deliver me,

O God, make haste to help me," he prays silently.

He opens his eyes. His friends are all reclining against trees or lying around on the grass. Simon has lain down, his head pillowed by a smooth rock. They have retreated to this quiet meadow in a remote part of the golden city to escape the crowds for a little while.

All except Judas.

He has gone off by himself

He didn't say where he was going.

Chapter 21

The signs slipped past: Haynes. Mott. White Butte. The sky behind us yellowed with the sinking sun. Strips of wheat and summer fallow were broken by patches of Russian Olive and Chinese Elm. Some of the grass in the ditches had been mowed and baled. The smell of ripe alfalfa drifted in through the vents.

"He slipped on an icy street one December noon and couldn't get up in time to get out of the way of an oncoming car," I said. "The left headlight met his right leg, splintering the headlight and bruising the leg."

The sunset was a joyous polka of purples, golds, and reds. The orange shadow of the sun hung like a copper penny stuck in the slot of an old red peanut machine—the kind with a glass top like the one that used to sit in my father's service station.

"It threw him down beneath the left rear wheel. The wheel thumped over his eight-year-old head."

"The blow didn't kill the boy, but he lay unconscious in the hospital with a broken skull for ten days while doctors speculated whether he would live or die—and whether he would ever return to normal consciousness."

"He awakened in the pre-Christmas haze, though, his mind clear and his memory intact."

'He stayed in the hospital until March. His mother came to see him every day. He had never been away from home for so long, and he could hardly wait to see her face each day. He hated watching her leave each night.

"As January gave way to February and Valentine's Day appeared on the horizon, he procured an empty olive jar from the housekeepers and set to work making his mother a special Valentine."

The sun was gone now. I switched on my headlights against the dusk.

"He carefully cut pieces of construction paper and drew flowers and butterflies on them. He colored them purple, red, yellow, blue, and green. Each day he hid his project when she came to visit, only to take it out again after she left each night.

"And when all the pieces were cut and properly colored, he carefully pasted them onto the jar, creating a flower vase made beautiful in his eyes by the labor of his love."

Shadehill. The green sign slid past. The arrow pointed south: Lemmon straight ahead. We pulled up over a hill as traffic thickened near the ballpark. The old wooden fences were gone now, but I remembered how they used to loom larger than those in Hettinger. They had bright signs painted on them advertising local merchants, looking so close when you stood in the batter's box—but they were really pretty far away. Nothing I ever hit came close to reaching them.

Chapter 22

The Will of God is becoming clearer to him now.

The soldiers have not stood indifferently beside the buildings today. They have moved closer to him and to the crowds as they passed, their faces set, expressionless, and drawn. Their hands moved nervously to their swords, only to return nervously to their sides again.

He told stories about coins and sheep and children running away from home, but no one seemed to be truly listening. The crowd was restless. The scribes were out in full force, challenging every word he spoke.

Some of them held back, mingling with the crowds, and murmured things so quietly that he couldn't make out what they were saying. As they spoke, he noticed some of the crowd turn to stare at him, only to turn back to the murmurers once more.

Chapter 23

The Shadehill sign slipped past again. We began to wind our way up the hill, a mile or so out of town.

"Whatever became of that boy and his Valentine?" he said, leaning back in the seat and tilting his hat over his eyes.

The road leveled out on top of the hill and pointed west. The first stars twinkled low in the southwest.

"His heart was an overflowing furnace of love and pride on Valentine's Day when he handed it to her," I said.

"She accepted it with the special grace a mother is given to receive such gifts from her children. She took it home, and he forgot all about it. But later that spring, when he was at home playing in the quiet yard—the other kids were still at school; he couldn't go back that year—later that spring, he discovered the vase in the smoldering garbage can out in the alley behind the house.

"Parts of the colored paper were burnt away, and the jar beneath was brown and charred. His heart came up into his throat as he reached down into the barrel and gently took it out, holding it in his hands. He turned it over, looking at the blackened edges where the colored paper had been burnt away.

"He thought of taking it inside and repairing it, making it pretty again. But instead, he dropped it back into the smoldering barrel, fought back tears, and went off to play somewhere else."

We drove along in silence until the moon appeared and the dark sky held a thousand stars.

Chapter 24

His mind drifts backward to another day, to a yesterday that seems like a hundred years ago, although it has only been about a year—just a little more than a year ago. His mind drifts backward to the day he was baptized in the Jordan by John.

His mind pauses on John for a moment. He recalls how Herod had imprisoned John and served his head to Salome, the daughter of Herodias, on a silver platter because he had been captivated by her dance.

He is beginning to think that something similar might happen to him. He closes his eyes and prays:

"Be pleased, O God, to deliver me;
O Lord, make haste to help me."

Chapter 25

The moon and the stars brought back another night. It was so light out that I could have driven without headlights if I had wanted to.

"The moon floated high above us," I said, recalling the night when the moon and the stars had brought back memories. "The stars flickered, a million of them. The Harding County night was cut in two by the Milky Way."

"I was in the pickup with my uncle, excited. I didn't often get to ride in the pickup with him or anyone else that summer. I was too little, they said. But that night, he took me along.

"We were gliding along a trail cut into the prairie by decades of motor vehicles. We traveled east away from the place. Some of the heifers had been calving, and he had been checking on them day and night. He had seen one that looked like it was going to have some trouble.

"I was excited, but I tried not to chatter too much. My uncle was like his brother, my father—a quiet man. He didn't have many words, and the ones he had, he used carefully. He seldom wasted any of them.

"So I sat in the pickup and watched the stars and the dark prairie. It was a ways—three or four miles—to wherever we were going. And there were gates. He had to get out and open them.

"I wasn't strong enough to stretch the wires enough to release the wire loop, nor strong enough to stretch the wires tight enough to slip the loop back over the post again. He had to open and close them.

'After a while, he slowed the pickup and went off the tracks, weaving through the sagebrush. He leaned forward on the wheel and strained his eyes. I couldn't tell what he was looking for."

Chapter 26

Let those who seek my life be ashamed and altogether dismayed;

Let those who take pleasure in my misfortune draw back and be disgraced.

David's words seem to fit the restless soldiers, the wearisome scribes, and the fickle crowds. It seems as though everybody in the world is starting to turn against him—even some of his best friends.

Let those who say to me, "Aha!" and gloat over me turn back, because they are ashamed.

These words give him pause.

Chapter 27

"There she is," he said as he turned the pickup and slowed to a quiet halt. He got out. I couldn't see 'her' yet, though. He started walking back through the sagebrush. I got out and ran beside him. Then I saw the heifer lying on her side. As I got closer, I saw a leg or two sticking out behind. The calf was coming out wrong. It was stuck—and probably dead.

"He went back to the pickup and came back with a rope. He performed a uterine survey with veterinary expertise and tried to turn the calf around. I watched, but I tried not to say anything. He looped the rope around the calf's legs and rose and walked back to tie the other end to the bumper. He told me to stand back. He got inside, started the engine, and put it into its lowest gear, slowly disengaged the clutch, and started to roll forward.

"The rope became taut. The heifer's legs shot out, and she bawled as the pickup dragged her a bit. Then the head came, and the body, and the blood. I was jumping around, waving my arms, but he didn't pay much attention to me. He had turned his head as he drove, his right arm draped over the back of the seat. He knew what was happening and when. He had done that very thing many times in his life, alone, before. He didn't need me.

"He halted the pickup, backed it up to loosen the rope, stopped the engine, and got out and walked back to the heifer and her calf. I stayed back. I knew I wasn't supposed to bother him or get in his way. He doctored the heifer. He removed the placenta from the calf, just in case, unhooked the rope, and rolled it up in his hand as he walked back to the pickup to unhook it. He laid it in the back of the pickup and walked around to the driver's side and got in. I ran around to the other side and hopped in.

"He started the pickup, glanced back at the heifer and her dead calf, and started forward. "I hope she makes it," he said as we began to drive towards the far-off lights of the place."

White Butte. The red lights of a patrol car sliced through the night. I let up on the gas with a jerk and looked down at the speedometer, settling in at exactly 55. He sat up and looked around. He saw the patrol car before I pointed. He looked over at me then slouched back down and closed his eyes.

The driver of the car the patrolman had stopped was sitting in the passenger seat. We passed and started into the night darkness over the railroad tracks into North Dakota.

"Well done, good and faithful servant," he said.
I wasn't sure who he was talking about. Or what.

Chapter 28

But if what he feels is going to happen to him soon really does happen, perhaps those who are ganging up on him will be ashamed. He doesn't know for sure. He decides not to think about it.

The windmill of his memory begins to spin, pumping up more of the psalm.

Chapter 29

"We carried his casket to the rack and rolled it above the grave out at Ladner in 1979," I said as we passed the Highway 8 turnoff and headed west again. "I stood back with the other pallbearers. The May wind bit my neck and ruffled through my unprotected hair.

"In sure and certain hope of the resurrection to eternal life," the pale, young pastor read. The women in the first row huddled close to one another and to their men, trying to cover their legs. Someone from behind bent down and wrapped a sweater around the widow's..

"'...earth to earth, ashes to ashes, dust to dust,'" he continued.

My father stood beside his brother's grave, head tilted, hat in hand. He was wearing a brown, western-style leisure suit. He looked so small.

Suddenly, we were driving out to Ladner from Bowman in our black Chevrolet. We pulled off onto an approach to check a tire or something. A rattlesnake was sunning itself on the gravel. My father quickly opened the trunk and took out a short piece of chain. He approached the snake cautiously. We stood back. The snake coiled up on the gravel, hissing, rattling, as he circled it. Every few seconds, he would bring the chain down. The snake would pull back, and the chain would bring up bits of dust and broken rock. Then the snake would settle back into striking position, rattling harder than ever. My father would quickly pull the chain back and start circling again. The battle went on until the snake lay twitching, dead upon the gravel. My father, sweating at the forehead and temples, put the chain back into the trunk.

But he wasn't sweating as he stood there beside his brother's grave in the chill May wind. His thin hair was uncovered, and his wrinkled hands were at his sides.

"'The Lord bless him and keep him,'" the pastor read on.

My mind tilted as I gazed at him, and I saw him twelve years old, cap in hand, ruddy face scrubbed to a shine, standing beside his father's grave as they lowered the casket into the ground. I couldn't tell whether he was crying or not.

Paper rattled

Lightly as he unwrapped a stick of gum. "'...and make his
face shine on him,'" the pastor continued.

Lilacs his mother planted grow wild upon that grave now, and she sleeps beside him again. I was there with him for her in 1961.

"'...and be gracious to him,'" the pastor read.

One day, I knew, a grave would be opened up there for him. And I would have to stand where he was standing.

"'...and look upon him with favor,'" the pastor said. Maybe then I'd be a man.

"'...and give him peace. Amen.'"

A faintly familiar scent filled the car.

"What kind of gum is that you're chewing?" I said. "Cinnamon," he answered. "Want a piece?"

I held out my hand.

Chapter 30

Let all who seek you rejoice and be glad in you;

let those who love your salvation say forever, "Great is the Lord!"

The clouds part for a moment, and sunlight trickles through the branches. His closed eyelids redden and seem almost transparent.

He feels for a moment like a child he saw that morning, tucked into a piece of cloth tied around a woman's waist. The child had been sleeping, rocked by its mother's gentle motion, its tiny head nestled against the softness of her breast.

The sun disappears, and his eyelids darken. The rest of the Psalm comes.

"But as for me, I am poor and needy,

come to me speedily, O God.

You are my helper and my deliverer; O Lord, do not tarry."

He is sure something dreadful is going to happen to him soon, and he is sure that God is the only one who can get him out of it.

"Great is the Lord!" he says, but he wonders why it has to be Judas.

Chapter 31

We had just passed Reeder. We were heading out to Harding County for the day. I saw a hawk beside a dead rabbit on the road up ahead, pecking away at exposed entrails. It flapped its huge wings and lifted slowly up as I came over the hill.

It circled and descended again after I had passed. It landed on the side of the road I had just traveled, opposite the dead rabbit, and began its slow walk back over to its dinner.

"One December, when new snow lay on the hills south of Hettinger," I said, "my brother and I were out hunting jackrabbits. I was walking slowly along when I saw, out of the corner of my eye, something move in the snow off to my right. My brother had gone off to the left, over the hill. I turned. The startled jackrabbit began to run.

"I twirled and pulled the firing pin back on the single-shot .22 and fired, in a single motion, without aiming, almost from the hip. My brother came running. 'I think you hit him,' he said.

"We trailed the path of bloody snow over the hill, down the draw, and up the side of the next hill. We came upon it, exhausted, twitching, bleeding, dying—its eyes shining—about a quarter of a mile away. My brother lifted his rifle and butted it down on the rabbit's head. It stretched out silent then on the red, red snow."

In the distance, in the rearview mirror, another car approached. The hawk would have to rise again.

"Victims," I thought, as we came over the next hill and I saw the bones of Gascoyne rising up out of the prairie.

Chapter 32

A familiar smell wafts through the air. The priests are back in the temple, burning their cinnamon incense again. He breathes the sweetness deeply in.

He opens his eyes and looks around. Peter and James are sitting with their backs against the same tree, their chins riding on their chests, napping. Simon lies on his side with his head upon a rock, eyes closed, too. Philip is stretched out on his stomach on the grass, asleep, with his head cradled in his folded arms.

Bartholomew, Matthew, Andrew, and the other James are strewn out on the grass, napping as well. So is Thomas, his back against another tree. And Judas. The other Judas is still gone. All are sleeping, except John. John is sitting on a rock nearby, beaming like the sun. He has been waiting for him to open his eyes for a long time.

When their eyes meet, John blurts out in a loud, excited whisper, "Can you smell the cinnamon, Jesus?" Jesus nods and smiles. John's eyes shine, and he grins from ear to ear. Jesus looks away from him, up into the branches of the pomegranate tree.

"Climb up there and get a branch, John," he says. "We'll need one for tomorrow."

Chapter 33

I drove on in silence. He was stretched out on the seat beside me, his head tilted back, his eyes closed. We passed Scranton and Buffalo Springs, drove through Bowman, and continued past the elevator at Griffin. At Rhame, I turned south.

"She was there the night I regained consciousness," I said as we passed Bethany. They were up on the roof, fixing the steeple.

"I don't remember her then. I don't remember anyone from that time. But I do remember her on other nights, sitting in the tan plastic-covered chair beside the nightstand. The room was lit only by that dim pole lamp with the tan metal shade that looked like an upside-down fruit bowl.

"I remember waking and seeing her there, quietly knitting, or crocheting, or reading. When I stirred, she came to me. She stroked my cheeks and asked how I was feeling and if I needed anything. She brought me water to drink and tucked the covers back up around my shoulders if I had tossed them off in sleep.

"Sometimes she lifted my wounded head, fluffed the pillow, and laid it gently back down on the cool side. And sometimes I screamed while I slept, tormented by nightmares of the accident from which I couldn't be awakened. She picked me gently up, wrapped me in a blanket, and rocked me in her arms while I tossed and screamed.

"For many days of my life, she is the only person I can remember. She sat beside my bed and watched me every night until the doctors said I was out of danger and she could go."

I looked over at him. He was laid back, still, his eyes closed. He had picked up the hat that had been lying in the back seat, put it on, and pulled it down over his eyes.

"She looked like Jesus and smelled like cinnamon to me," I said.

We drove on in silence until the pavement ended and the gravel began. The roughness made him stir. He sat up, pushed his hat back, and looked out.

"I knew that was you," he said.

My brow wrinkled. "Knew who was me?" I asked.

"The Valentine boy," he answered.

Chapter 34

Thursday night. The sun had dropped off the edge of the earth hours ago. The moon and stars had appeared.

The air of Jerusalem was filled with the odor of burning fat. The priests were still hard at work, slaughtering the pilgrim sacrifices and throwing the fat of the animals onto the fire in the middle of the altar.

He and his friends reclined on cushions around a low table in the room he had procured for them to celebrate the Passover Feast. They were but a small handful of the more than hundred thousand Passover pilgrims gathered in other rooms just like it in the golden city tonight.

He had found a lamb, had it slaughtered, and received the carcass back. He had found someone to fold it over a stick of pomegranate wood and someone to cook it in their oven for him.

"The Lord has need of it," was all he had to say.

Chapter 35

We approached the butte and curved west before we got to where Karinen used to be. The magnificent old scoria-covered Horseshoe Bend up against the butte, going west out of Karinen, looked from the new road like a trail little boys had made to drive their toys upon.

"July 4, 1952," I said. "None of us could have dreamed that the telephone would bring the news it brought that day.

"I was at home with my brothers, my sister, and Jesse, an infant cousin. An aunt from Minneapolis was with us, too. My father, mother, uncle, and another aunt—Jesse's parents—had gone off to Lemmon to see the Petrified Wood Park.

"It was a hot summer day. Jesse stood diapered but bare otherwise in the dusty sunlight of the doorway leading out to the porch. The excitement of company, relatives from a distant state whom we didn't see too often, filled the house."

We rattled south up over the cattle guard on the top of the butte. Down below, the Thune place came into view.

"It rang about an hour after they left," I continued.

Chapter 36

They have finished the first course of the Passover Meal. The taste of wine, lamb, the bitter Passover herbs, and harosheth lingers in his mouth. The lamb is almost gone, and the herbs are too. Bits of harosheth remain in the dipping dish.

Soon it will be time to sing and recite the Passover history. Soon it will be time to lift the second cup. But he isn't in any hurry. His friends are grouped together in twos and threes, talking to each other. All except Judas, who has withdrawn even more deeply into himself this night. He reclines alone, staring.

He rehearses the rest of the night in his heart.

Chapter 37

The road past the Thune place was oiled down. They started doing that after oil was struck on their land. There was no dust.

"There had been an accident, they said," I said. "My parents were both in surgery, they said. My uncle was in the hospital, they said. Aunt Carrie was dead, they said."

"My other aunt spent the rest of the afternoon crying between phone calls to relatives and to the authorities in Lemmon, trying to get more details. Slowly, the details came in. As my uncle was approaching Lemmon, an elderly man headed for Shadehill Dam to go fishing—bamboo poles strapped to the door handles of his car—turned off about a quarter of a mile too soon, apparently without looking, toward the opposite ditch, right into the path of my uncle's red Ford convertible.

Up ahead, the road curved west again. I let up on the gas. "He slammed into the old fisherman's car," I continued.

A sloping hillside beyond the next curve, with rocks jutting out of the grass behind the barbed wire in places, came into view. "The old man died instantly," I said, slowing more.

"The impact of the collision pushed the motor of my uncle's car into the front seat, passenger side, crushing my aunt. My uncle slammed against the steering wheel, breaking ribs and puncturing a lung. He would be released from the hospital in a day or so. Then my parents came out of surgery. They had been in the back seat. The doctors had worked for hours putting my father's broken arm and leg and neck and my mother's broken arms and legs back together again. They were listed in critical condition."

We curved west. "There's where the homestead used to be," I said, motioning to the left with my head. "Just over the hill."

He sat up and looked out over the vacant acres. The top of a single tree showed above the crest of the first hill—Grandma's tree.

"Where was the windmill?" he asked as the car came out of the curve.

"I don't know," I said. "He never told me." A picture of my grandfather, atop the shack tinkering with the binder reel, struggled in my brain.

Chapter 38

How shall I repay the Lord for all the good things he has done for me?

The words flow like honey inside of him, evoking pictures of his mother and of the birds, and memories of stories he had heard. He remembers especially the story his father first told him about how people were once delivered out of slavery in Egypt by passing through the sea.

How shall I repay the Lord for all the good things he has done for me?

Chapter 39

He stretched back out in the seat and pulled the hat back down over his eyes.

"Relatives poured in the next day," I said. "Uncle John said he drove his Oldsmobile a hundred miles an hour all the way from Minneapolis. Arnold and Selma from Harding County, Ed and Laura, and others from Miles City came. They stood outside on the driveway in the July sunshine, discussing in hushed tones — ones we weren't supposed to hear—what they were going to do with us.

"Offers were made for some of us to go out to Minneapolis to live. They knew my parents were in extreme danger, and not even the doctors knew whether they would live or die. My Harding County uncle prevailed.

"We were not to be so separated. He would take my older brother and me with him out to Harding County. Gail and Curt would go to Miles City with Ed and Laura.

"It was a quiet ride out here to Harding County. No one dared talk much about what had happened or about what might happen next."

Ladner came into view. Sheep were in the road at the Stenerson place, and chickens pecked in the yard. I slowed for the sheep.

"Over the next weeks, news came to us from Lemmon in bits and pieces. We couldn't go see them, though. Their condition remained critical.

"Uncle Steve had been released from the hospital and had gone back to Minneapolis with his brother, John, and his son, Jesse, to bury his wife."

He sat up as I braked and swerved to avoid a chicken that decided at the last moment that the other side of the road was much more exciting than the one it was on. I steadied the car again. He glanced back at the chicken hightailing it through the grass.

The long, low post office, store, and home of Lou and Lenora Gotfredson—the entire population of Ladner except for the Stenersons—grew larger. Up the street, the schoolhouse stood to the left, and farther up still, on the right, the church stood silent in the morning light.

"Ladner," I said.

He glanced up at the church and schoolhouse and stared out at the lonely little store.

Chapter 40

I will lift the cup of salvation and call upon the name of the Lord.

The cup of salvation—that will be the second cup they lift tonight. Bartholomew has been designated to ask the ceremonial question, "Why is this night different from all other nights?" Then the singing and the recitation will begin.

He begins to think of new things. He looks down at the cup in front of him, at the bread beside it on the table.

"I will fulfill my vows to the Lord in the presence of all his people. Precious in the sight of the Lord is the death of his servants."

His friends chatter on.

Chapter 41

Ladner disappeared behind the hills.

"That summer, my cousin Florence, five years older than I, told me that if I counted the stars in the Big Dipper every night and made the same wish, that wish would come true," I said. "Every night, I went out and found the Big Dipper and wished harder than I had ever wished before that my parents would get better and that life would return to normal again."

He stirred in his seat. I began to look for the sign.

"Eventually, the news came that they were taken off the critical list, that they had been moved, and that they were now in a room together," I continued.

Gunderson—white sign with red letters; the small arrow pointed north. I slowed and turned.

"We went to Lemmon to see them," I said. "They lay in hospital beds framed above and at the corners with galvanized pipe. Ropes with weights were attached to their bodies, suspended on pulleys from the pipes. Metal pins pierced their knees, anchoring the ropes."

Far off to the northwest, the gray buildings of the place came into view. We crossed the cattle guard and began to wind toward it, through the rough land.

"My father's head was in a canvas strap. He couldn't turn it," I said.

Two deer stared up at us from the bottom of the gray slope of a bad land break. The scoria lifted up red dust in the rearview mirror.

Chapter 42

There is no way out of it now. He has tried to live a perfect Hebrew life. Now he must prepare to die a perfect Hebrew death.

He doesn't know when, though. Or how.

"O Lord, I am your servant, and the child of your handmaid," he says. "You have freed me from my bonds.

(His mother's face.)

"I will offer you the sacrifice of thanksgiving and call upon the name of the Lord.

I will fulfill my vows to the Lord in the presence of all his people, in the courts of the Lord's house, in the midst of you, O Jerusalem."

The words echo in his mind.

"In the presence of all his people. In the courts of the Lord's house. In the midst of you, O Jerusalem."

The words sting.

Chapter 43

We rattled over the cattle guard into the place. The Aeromotor was silent. The pointed roof of the weathered barn jutted above the newer tin building. Off to the right, gray garages stood. And behind them, I knew, were the chicken coops and granaries, rows of trees, haystacks, and beyond them the pastures where I used to ride Frosty out to get the cows—Mud Butte, and beyond, the sand hills that shifted locations over the years in the wind. Sagebrush. Prairie chickens. Rattlesnakes.

We pulled up at the white frame house. I shut down the car.

"What became of all those people?" he asked as he leaned around and over the seat to replace the hat. A whirl of dust came around the corner of the barn.

"Uncle Steve remarried and had another family," I said. "Jesse grew up and lives in Wisconsin now. He is married and has children of his own. Uncle John died of kidney failure. I helped carry Uncle Arnold out to the Ladner cemetery a couple of years ago. My brothers and sister and parents live in Washington. My father still limps."

I opened the door. We got out.

"My parents recovered enough to be brought home that November," I continued. "Another aunt, Marie, came from Hallock, Minnesota, to nurse and take care of them and look after us," I said as I raised my fist to knock upon the widow's door. "For a while, things got to be the way they used to be again."

Chapter 44

There's no turning back now. If the Lord wants him to die a precious death in his sight, he will die a precious death in his sight.

He is the Lord's servant.

He looks down at the lamb bones and the dish of harosheth. The taste of the bitter herbs returns for a moment, and he can still faintly smell the smell of burning fat. But no cinnamon. The smoke, the wine, the spices, the herbs, the fruits, the bread, and the nuts have drowned out all other odors.

His friends chatter on and laugh. John is telling Peter and James about something he saw in the marketplace. His eyes shine, and his hands dance this way and that. Judas remains withdrawn, unmoved by it all. He can feel Judas' eyes upon him.

Chapter 45

After supper, we walked around the place. I remembered the big black Tom turkey Selma used to have, how it would run me down and stand on my chest; how we used to play "Beckon, Beckon, Who's got the Beckon?"—hiding on top of granaries, behind trees, and underneath machinery from whoever was "it."

On the western edge of the place, abandoned cars—rusted, windowless, and tireless—rested alongside pull-type combines and tractors with studded iron wheels that no longer turned. They were all beneath a row of trees. I used to walk the pasture beyond, collecting bones. There used to be a pile of them out here. They brought a few cents a pound in those days. Skulls and thigh bones were premium finds—heavy. Ribs were light and commonplace. The white pile was gone.

The hayloft of the barn was closed. For a moment, I stood up in the open door. Arnold was down below, quietly giving instructions. Selma was up in the chicken yard, gathering eggs, wearing a faded cotton dress, brown lace shoes with block heels, and her hair tied with a scarf.

They were quiet people, gentle people. They neither smoked nor drank, and they went to church all the time. Selma played the organ, and Arnold was on the council. How different we had been.

"When I was fifteen," I said, "a freshman in high school, a friend and I hooked up with some older kids and rode down to a party in the trees along the Grand River south of Hettinger." We walked through the bottom of the empty barn, past the empty stalls.

Frosty used to stand in one, patiently, while I cinched the saddle on. The sweet smell of hay and the sharp smell of manure filled the air, along with the scent of leather. Saddles rested on the wooden stall dividers, and dark bridles hung on nails on the back wall.

"It was dark and dusty," I continued. "Cars were everywhere. Beer was flowing freely, and other things were happening. It was rumored that some of the older couples had gone on up the river to swim without any clothes on."

I unhooked the bottom of the other divided door. The top half was hooked back against the wall. We went out into the open corral. I closed the bottom, and hooked it up again.

We passed between the barn and the tin building, then on into the adjoining gray lean-to. We walked out past the tin building and climbed up over the rough two-by-twelves into the next corral. The wooden water tank, which we sometimes used to strip down and swim in when it was hot, was underneath the adjacent fence, half in each corral, so that the cattle from both could drink from it. The cold, wet iron pipe ran out from the weathered pumphouse.

"Then I was in a car with my friend on the other side of the highway," I said. "I can't remember whose car it was or how we got there. We were feeling giddy from the beer, and we had acquired a half-pint of whiskey."

We entered the pumphouse.

"We sat there in the back seat and drank the whole thing down together, straight, laughing and joking and cheering each other on with wild drunken statements about being a 'man'."

I put my hand on the galvanized ladder.

"Let's climb up," I said.

"You first," he replied.

"Did you ever make it?" he asked as we came out onto the platform into the open air.

"Make what?" I asked.

"Being a man," he said.

Chapter 46

"I might as well not keep them waiting any longer," he thinks. "First, I must become a servant to my friends. Then I will break bread and lift the cup with them for the last time. Judas can go off to wherever it is he has to go and do whatever it is he has to do. And then I will go up into the garden for a while."

He turns to Peter, sitting near him, and says, "Go get me a bowl of water, Peter."

"What do you want a bowl of water for, Lord?" Peter asks.

"So I can wash your feet, Peter," Jesus answers.

Peter looks at him like he is crazy.

Chapter 47

We sat on the platform beneath the gray metal sunflower, gazing up at the bright stars and out across the dark prairie. Crickets chirped. A gray cat strolled across the corral and disappeared into the tin building where they used to milk. The cats would sit beside the stools, swishing their tails and licking their chops. Occasionally, a milker would tilt a teat in their hands and spray a stream into a waiting cat's face. The cat would turn and blink, startled at first, then sit and lick the whiteness from its whiskers.

"Ever play baseball?" I asked. The silence was palpable.

"I remember the last inning of the semi-final game in the State Class B High School Baseball Tournament, spring of 1959. We were playing a team that had entered the tournament on the strong arms of two brothers—one a right-handed pitcher, the other left-handed."

The Big Dipper tilted in the north, and the Milky Way spread wide and white across the middle of the sky. The lights from a distant car cut into the prairie darkness.

"The big right-hander had won the opening game for them, so we faced his left-handed brother the next day. It was the last inning. There were two outs, and the bases were empty. We were behind three to two. I stepped into the batter's box."

The low green and red stars seemed to be moving, almost dancing in the sky.

"I had had fairly good success against the left-hander that day. I had hit line drives my first two times up; one had dropped in for a single."

The galvanized windmill leg was cool against my back. Occasionally, a breeze pushed against the locked blades below, making the metal creak and the legs shiver.

"I could see the left-field fence, the ball I had just hit sailing over it, as I watched him wind up. I tightened my grip on the bat handle as he kicked."

"I was expecting a fastball or that flat curve again, so I wasn't at all ready when the ball floated by after I had swung—a crazy-looking knuckleball, the first one he'd thrown all day."

"I stepped out, rubbed dirt on my hands, looked out at him, and stepped back in. He kicked and threw. I swung in perfect time to his fastest pitch. The bat was already arcing over my opposite shoulder when the second knuckleball floated by. 'Strike Two!'"

"I stepped out and put more dirt on my hands, checking the bat for holes. I swung a couple of times, then stood back in. I knew he wouldn't dare throw that knuckleball three times in a row. I dug my back foot in. He kicked and threw. I guessed fastball."

"I had already finished my third swing when the third knuckleball floated by me as pretty as a butterfly."

The thin slice of quarter moon looked like a slit in the western sky. I wondered whether it was letting light in or out.

PART THREE

    Cool Rain

God, you who cause your grace to fall

like cool rain

upon the steaming sidewalks of our souls,

take our prayers:

take our prayers and gracefully transform

our fragile bodies,

so that what we want

and what we do

may please you.

Chapter 48

It's dark as midnight, but it's not even three o'clock in the afternoon yet. The sun went out three hours ago.

The end is near. Judas went and did what he had to do. The soldiers came for him while they were in the garden. The cock crowed as he stood before the governor.

Then came the angry crowds, the lashes, the soldiers with their fists and taunts and sticks and thorny crown—their mockery, their laughter, and their spit. Then the cross, stumbling, crawling, weak beneath its weight...to this hill. They stretched him out like a scarecrow upon it, nailed him down, and raised him up.

"King of the Jews," they mocked.

Chapter 49

The morning broke bright and serene. Meadowlarks sang on the cemetery fence. Sparrows hopped in Grandpa's lilacs.

G. H. Gunderson. Mathilde Gunderson. We walked on.

Arnold Gunderson. The bed beside him was vacant. Selma would sleep there soon. I wondered where my father's grave would be.

Martin Gunderson.

"I was seven years old when he died," I said, stopping at the marker. "He was a bachelor. I can remember seeing him only once before the funeral."

"He was a small man, wrinkled up like my father is now. He sat in another bachelor uncle's kitchen, at the white enamel table with Dad and Uncle Pete and me, and picked up blue Bicycles from the red and white checkered oilcloth and arranged them in his hand.

"I was too young to join in, but they laughed and drank and played cards together all afternoon." High overhead, the white contrails of B-52s from the airbase at Rapid City unwound as they flew on maneuvers.

"After a while, Uncle Pete brought out a paring knife, a new block of Velveeta cheese in a bright yellow box, and a box of saltine crackers, and laid them on the table. He opened another bottle of beer for each of them, shuffled the cards, and started to deal them out."

I squatted down and began to pull dandelions and creeping jenny out of the mound.

"He looked over at me and said, 'Why don't you cut some cheese for us and put it on those crackers?'"

I tried to polish the metal marker with my palm. Martin Gunderson.

"I opened the yellow box, took out the block, cut the slick wrapper, and peeled it back. I picked up the paring knife and laid it to the soft cheese. The slices were very uneven and much, much too thick in places, not nearly as pretty as I wanted them to be."

I picked off pebbles and threw them beyond the fence.

"I put them on the saltines and passed them around anyway, complaining about the knife. Then I cut another round," I said, standing up and straightening out my jeans and brushing my hands together. "They were as unpretty as the first. I was beginning to be discouraged. I passed them around and complained about the knife again.

"'I like the way you cut cheese,' Uncle Martin said as I started to cut another round.

'I like it thick like that.'

"I cut the next round more uneven," I said, looking away, "and even thicker in places."

A meadowlark sang on the corner post. A car slowed on the road below, as if its driver were trying to figure out who was up there and why. Then it picked up and moved on, too busy or too polite to stop and ask and see.

"I wonder who that was up at the graveyard this morning?" they would say at dinner, starting a guessing game that would last throughout the meal and beyond, into telephone conversations for the rest of the day.

Chapter 50

The pain is gone now. His back is raw from the lashes, with more flesh rubbing off every time he moves. Thorns pierce the skin of his skull, causing a puffy, numb tightness. One eye is almost swollen shut. His jaw is puffed out from the blows, and his lips are swollen too. He is thirsty.

If someone doesn't come and rescue him soon…

Chapter 51

"For a while after we grew up and started to move away, we tried to get together at Christmas for a reunion," I said. We pulled off the cemetery trail and onto the gravel road, headed east for Ladner.

"We would eat big meals, nibble on nuts cracked open with pliers when we couldn't find the nutcrackers, open presents, play cards, put together jigsaw puzzles, and drink wine and beer. And we always stayed up late, talking.

"One year, we were sitting in the living room—my dad, my older brother, and I. I was in my second year of college, starting to read a lot of books.

"I don't remember what we were talking about, but whatever it was, I was excited. I was trying to explain to them what I had read about it in books. They weren't impressed.

"'I don't see much sense in going to school if all you're going to learn how to do is read books,'" my father said. My brother agreed.

"I don't remember anything else anybody said after that."

He was laid back in the seat again, his eyes closed, covered with the hat. He didn't move. A bull stood menacingly in the ditch, free from the barbed wire for a moment. His white-faced red heifers and their calves grazed leisurely in the pasture, unimpressed. The car kicked up gravel and dust as we passed. The stone pieces rattled in the wheel wells and underneath the car.

Chapter 52

"My God, my God, why have you forgotten me,

And are so far from my cry and from the words of my distress"

He wants to cry out that beginning, but he is too weary, too weak, too thirsty. He is afraid his lips might crack.

"O' my God, I cry in the daytime but you do not answer;

by night as well, but I find no rest."

When had David ever cried out like that? When Saul was pursuing him? When he stood before Goliath? When Bathsheba's baby died? When Absalom strangled in the branches? When he lay dying himself, weak and old and cold, covered by warm maidens who tried to keep his body warm with theirs?

"You are the Holy One enthroned on the praises of Israel.

Our forefathers trusted in you; they trusted in you, and you delivered them."

(Abraham. Isaac. Jacob. His mother's face.)

"They cried out to you and were delivered.

They trusted in you and were not put to shame."

Chapter 53

The church was empty. The pews, altar, and lectern were gone. Someone had taken away the pews. The piano and the organ had been removed to the new church over by the cemetery. It looked smaller than it used to be.

He had wandered into the sanctuary, standing in the middle of the aisle, looking around. I halted in the narthex. There was just enough room behind the door for a casket. On the other side, steep steps descended down into the rock-walled basement. Men used to stand out here before church and talk.

I looked at the casket space, empty now.

"One wet spring day this place was full of people," I called. He turned. "It was my first funeral. The casket was open here," I pointed, "for the mourners to pass by as they filed out. My mother stood behind me in line, holding onto my shoulders.

"I looked down at the black corduroy rubber aisle runner that used to run where you're standing now. I wished I could get down and run my hands sideways across it like I used to when the church was empty. We moved up. Just before we arrived at the casket, my mother leaned down and whispered nervously to me, 'Look sad. It's the last time you'll ever see him.'

"I glanced in. "I like the way you cut cheese, he said, without opening his eyes or moving his lips. "I like it thick like that."

"We moved on."

A wind had come up. It whistled across the prairie, through the vacant steeple, and out around the corners of the building. The door rattled.

Chapter 54

"But as for me, I am a worm and no man,

scorned by all and despised by the people."

He opens one swollen eye and looks out at the soldiers and the spectators. Some are pointing at him. One spits. Another reaches down to pick up something.

All who see me laugh me to scorn, they curl their lips

and wag their heads, saying, "He trusted in the Lord;

let him deliver him; let him rescue him if he delights in him."

(He thinks he hears the words.)

Yet you are he who took me out of the womb and kept me safe upon my mother's breast.

His mother's face appears again. He looks out and thinks he sees her standing there. He tries to move his lips, but he doesn't know if anything comes out. He closes his eyes. Darkness. And the Psalm.

Chapter 55

We rattled up over the cattle guard, past the schoolhouse, and down towards the curve.

"One May night," I said, "I was at another party down by another river. Dust filtered through the trees. Someone had started a fire. Flames illuminated the nearby keg. Laughter came out of the trees, and loud talk."

We curved east.

"Somewhere Anita was with another guy. When she appeared, a cup of beer in one hand, she was hanging onto him with the other. She was looking up at him, laughing. I filled my paper cup again."

Karinen. The pool table used to have gashes in the green sewn up with fat thread by the owner with the glass eye. The balls bumped over them. The Planter's Peanut packages under the glass counter had usually been visited by mice.

"Someone came and asked me if I wanted to go along," I said. We curved south.

"They were going into town to get another keg. The car was full. We drove up to the liquor store that I had visited nearly every night for the past three months. The driver got out and went inside. The others chattered and laughed. I didn't feel like laughing. I didn't feel like talking. I wanted to be alone.

"'Can I get out?' I said to the passenger in the front seat, pressing her shoulder. She opened the door, slid forward, and pulled the seat back. I was free. I walked over to the railroad tracks. I walked up between them and looked down into the darkness. I started to run."

We curved east again, then south towards Rhame.

Chapter 56

I have been entrusted to you ever since I was born.

You were my God when I was still in my mother's womb.

Be not far from me, for trouble is near, and there is none to help.

Many young bulls encircle me, strong bulls of Bashan surround me.

They open wide their jaws at me, like a ravening and roaring lion.

He tries to lift his head and open his eyes. One won't open. The other blurs. Through its fog, the soldiers look menacing. The people like their lips and open up their mouths.

"Let us not tear it…"

Pain returns to his hands and feet. His back throbs. His head and face sting.

Chapter 57

Bethany Church. They were still working on the steeple. One of the workers hailed us as we passed, and I honked.

"Two a.m.," I continued. The sun's rays slanted in the purple west. "It was raining. My hair and clothes were wet. An acquaintance who had been at the party strolled by as if in a dream. He asked me what I was doing.

"I was sitting in the middle of the sidewalk across the street from the house where I roomed. I didn't know how I got there. I didn't know where I'd been. It was over two miles by road and rail back to the liquor store. I must have left there two hours ago. The last thing I remembered was looking down the tracks and starting to run.

"I didn't answer him. I got up and weaved my way over to the house in the rain.

"The days ran together after that. School finally got out. I didn't want to go back anymore. I didn't want to go anywhere.

"I took a bus out to Washington to be with my brother for the summer and try to find a job." The scoria buttes of Rhame appeared, shadowed in the sunset.

"The job didn't work out, so I came back home early, broke. I began to look forward to September."

A jackrabbit shot out of the clover in front of me. I braked to avoid it, then sped up again.

"Before snow covered the campus that fall, a friend arranged a meeting for me with his girlfriend's roommate.

"I went up to the dorm with him. It was six o'clock on a Sunday night in early October. He went upstairs to ring for his friend.

"She came down to meet him." I turned on the headlights.

"I stood at the bottom of the landing, alone. I couldn't believe her friend would come. I had seen her from afar last year and decided she was much too fine for me.

"Suddenly, the blur of her blue dress appeared at the top of the steps—and her eyes. Her surprised look stunned me for a moment.

"It was Noel.

"We had never met before.

"We walked down to the café with her friend and mine and drank hot chocolate. I smoked a chain of Marlboros and chattered excitedly about nothing—the moon, F. Scott Fitzgerald—without looking at her.

"Then we walked back to the dorm.

"A few weeks later, she was gone—our relationship severed by a note delivered in silence at the Student Union one night.

"I started looking for the tracks." A red octagon arose ahead—a stop sign. "But then she came back."

The car slowed to a stop as I looked both east and west.

"We moved on," I said as we pulled onto Highway 12 and headed east, away from Rhame. "Together."

The stars were beginning to come out, and the thin slice of moon had risen again. The car was silent, and the prairie lay vacant except for the dark form of a distant windmill.

"I had a girl like that once," he said after a long silence.

"Really?" I answered. "What was her name?"

"Church," he said.

"Church? That's a funny name for a girl," I said.

"Not as funny as Christmas," he answered.

"Noel," I corrected.

"Noel," he repeated softly.

We drove on through the vacant prairie night as windmills rose like skeletons from out of the dark landscape.

"You said 'had,'" I finally said after turning his revelation over in my mind several times. "What do you mean 'had'? Isn't she your girl anymore? What happened to her?"

It was a long time before he finally measured out a response.

"I think she fell in love with herself," he said quietly, "and forgot about me."

Chapter 58

I am poured out like water; all my bones are out of joint. My heart within my breast is melting wax. My mouth is dried out like a potsherd, my tongue sticks to the roof of my mouth; and you have laid me in the dust of the grave.

He feels something wet on his lips. And bitter. Had he cried out? Had his lips cracked?

Packs of wild dogs close me in, and gangs of evildoers circle around me; they pierce my hands and my feet.

I can count all my bones. They stare and gloat over me; they divide my garments among them; they cast lots for my clothing.

Be not far away, O Lord; you are my strength; hasten to help me. Save me from the sword, my life from the power of the dog. Save me from the lion's mouth, my wretched body from the horns of wild bulls.

Chapter 59

"And it came to pass in those days, that there went out a decree from Caesar Augustus..." The words startled me. I looked over at him, wondering if perhaps he had spoken them. But he was laid back, his hat down over his eyes again, and silent. I looked out into the path cut by my headlights in the prairie darkness. Suddenly, I recognized the voice. It was my father. He considered it his Christian duty every Christmas Eve to sit in the chair, beside the fuel oil stove with the kerosene lamp lighted atop, and recite the lofty cadences of the Christmas story from the King James Luke to us. I relaxed and let him speak.

"And there were in the same country shepherds abiding in the fields..." A picture came with the words—a young man in dark clothes, a dark hat, sitting out on the step of his sheepwagon at night. Coyotes howled.

He looked over his sheep as he tapped the Bull Durham out of the white bag onto the thin white paper folded between the fingers of his other hand. He licked it, smoothed it shut, twisted the ends, put one end between his lips, pulled a farmer match out of his shirt pocket, struck it on the step, and a blaze of light illuminated his face. He cradled the match and cigarette in his dark brown hands, puffed, then waved the match out as the smoke came.

"For unto you is born this day in the city of David..." The words came slowly, roughly, from deep places, with labored pronunciations. I heard sheep bleating, lambs and babies crying, coyotes howling, and angels singing in his voice.

I began to wonder if I would ever be as close to him as I was on those nights, as the lights of Bowman spread like candles across the prairie silence. They lit up another memory. I saw a man come riding over the hills beyond the corral on his horse. A woman, a boy, a girl, and a small child stood waiting, watching, in the dusk in front of their house. The sheepherder was coming home.

"And they came with haste, and found Mary and Joseph, and the babe lying in the manger."

Chapter 60

The shock has worn off. The pain is back. His lips are drier than ever.

"I will declare your name to my brethren in the midst of the congregation; I will praise you. Praise the Lord, all who fear him; stand in awe of him, O offspring of Israel; all you of Jacob's line, give thanks.

"For he does not despise nor abhor the poor in their poverty. Neither does he hide his face from them; when they cry to him, he hears them."

He lifts his bruised head and opens his dry lips.

"My God...My God...Why...Have...You...Forgotten...Me?" he cries. He bows his head.

And then he is silent.

Chapter 61

As we passed Buffalo Springs, I saw Cornelius Schaff, somewhere between ten and twenty, turning in on his faded red McCormick tractor. Later, I saw him again, coming down the gravel of Highway 12 from the west in a cloud of dust, turning as he did almost every day that summer—into my father's little service station.

He looked like a king perched high on the tractor seat, his round helmet shading his dark eyes. He climbed down as I scrambled up onto the hood, removed the gas cap, and held the nozzle while the numbers on the red, white, and blue glass- crowned pump spun and fuel rushed in.

Cornelius went inside and pulled a huge bottle of Pepsi-Cola ("Pepsi-Cola hits the spot! Nickel, nickel, it's a lot!") dripping up out of the red cooler. He paid my father with a quarter and received two dimes back in change, laughing and chattering as he slipped his fortune into his overall pocket like a grown man.

He kidded with us when he came back out. We begged him to take us along.

He climbed back onto the seat, adjusted his helmet, leaned over the black steering wheel, grinned, and pushed the starter until the lid on top of the upright muffler stopped flapping and stayed open. Then he clutched and shifted, waved, and sped off to the east in another cloud of dust.

One day, though, his little red tractor slipped on loose gravel while turning off Highway 12 into Buffalo Springs. It rolled over and crushed him beneath its weight. He never came back after that.

I looked hard into the ditch at the turnoff where it happened and wondered how—and why.

The image of Cornelius faded into memory as a small blue book tumbled out of my mental graveyard: Rules of Order for Everyday Life by Henry Slade Goff. It opened.

The purple stamp on the frontal page announced: G.H. Gunderson. Ladner, S. Dak. The page turned: First Edition. 1912. Webb Publishing. St. Paul, Minnesota.

That was that was two years after my father came out west. He had given me this book after telling me about the windmill.

The subtitle promised: Civil Government Illustrated and Made Plain. The book transformed in my mind into a small white story-and-a-half frame house behind twin trees flanking a brick sidewalk I had once laid upon a lawn I planted years ago. I imagined myself going through its front door.

The ten-by-sixteen living room was the original floor of the house. Beyond it was a door leading to the kitchen. My mother was cooking inside. She heard me enter and came to the door with a wooden ladle in her hands.

"Oh! It's you," she said. "I thought maybe it was Dad. He should be home pretty quick." She went back to her work as I laid my coat on the couch and passed through into the slope-ceilinged lean-to kitchen.

"Oh! You have a new jacket!" she exclaimed as she moved over to touch my herringbone tweed.

"I've had it for two years," I replied while moving to sit at the round oak table opposite the stove in one of the swivel desk chairs.

"Really? I haven't seen it before," she said admiringly. "It sure looks nice."

"I wish Dad had one like that," she added before turning back to her stove while chattering about her friends ("Bob and Norma were in this morning with eggs; Lois is coming over this afternoon—she wants me to cut out a dress for her; Deborah just called—she said she saw you at the hospital.") and about family out west ("There's a letter from Sylvette on the window; Scott joined the army; Curt's are moving again; Gail and Lewis went to the Rose Bowl.").

She is a short, four feet eleven inch, gray-haired Ukrainian woman of peasant stock my father met during the Depression when he and his brother Pete were herding sheep in northern Minnesota. After forty years on these plains, her peasant heritage (and mine) felt remote and mysterious to me—like her mother's delicate Easter eggs.

Belle Iris Sopiwnik—Gunderson now.

My father came in through the back door shuffling up its step with his familiar limp. When he saw me, he broke into a grin and said "Hallo" in his pinched nasal voice. He took off his cap and hung it on a nail by the door—a quarter-century older than his father when he died—five-nine and brown from seventy-five years under Dakota sun. The skin of his skull showed through thinning hair above his wrinkled face as he removed his glasses to wipe them with his handkerchief—the veins protruding from his thin brown hands.

He went into the bathroom to wash while my mother brought steaming food from the stove to our neatly set table ("Did you finish out at Walch's today?"). We sat down to eat as she asked whether we needed this or that.

I asked about fishing, their health, and where he'd been working. They answered each question—sometimes simultaneously—but usually he deferred so she could speak.

When dinner ended, we cleared the table as coffee was poured and drunk. It was time for me to leave. They followed me to the door where she piled magazines into my arms ("For Noel...and ADAMS COUNTY RECORDS...there's something about Gretchen or Josh in there—4-H or basketball.").

"Goodbye! We'll see you."

"Ask Noel if she..."

"I'll call tomorrow..."

The door opened behind me—and closed.

We bumped up over their rough driveway before halting beside their Chinese Elm hedge as I leaned forward over my steering wheel—the headlights exposing scraggly Ponderosa branches three or four feet apart—the trees I'd brought home from work one summer to plant in front of their garage.

"Rules of Order for Everyday Use," I murmured aloud before leaning back to shut off my car engine while pushing in its lights.

I glanced over at him, sitting upright now—hat pushed back—as he looked directly at me.

I pulled my keys from their ignition slot before slipping them into my jeans pocket as I reached for my door handle.

"Let's go inside," I said.

Chapter 62

One of the soldiers gets up and walks over to see what's going on. "It looks like this one in the middle is finally dead," he calls out. "Better poke him first to make sure," one of the officers answers. The soldier lifts his spear and pierces. Blood and water trickle out.

"He's dead," he calls.

The others rise and come to help him take the bodies down. They take the two bandits first, break their legs, and toss them in a heap on the ground. Then they take Jesus down.

"We better not break his legs," the officer cautions. "Those friends of his might still be around. We don't want any more trouble."

They lay him out on the ground beside the bandits. Two are ordered to stay and watch. Joseph of Arimathea arrives with servants and permission to take the body. They wrap it in burial spices and a linen cloth and carry it off to a tomb in the nearby garden. They take it inside, carefully lay it out on the burial bench, and leave.

The odor of myrrh, aloes, and cinnamon fills their nostrils as they roll the stone over the entrance.

"Did you smell the cinnamon?" one of the servants blurts out, unable to bear the silence, as they hurry home to the Sabbath rest.

Chapter 63

Saturday morning. 5 a.m. Soon the sun would pour in through the east kitchen window. I stood before the stove in the corner, watching the bacon sizzle in the pan. I whistled, thinking I would be back in Reeder with Noel and the kids by noon.

I thought I heard a stirring behind me, thought I heard him come in and sit down.

"One day when I was out mowing my lawn," I said, "I discovered two small bushes laden with yellow roses out among the chokecherries in the backyard."

I turned the bacon.

"When I returned to the garage with the mower, I brought a pair of shiny tinsnips with yellow plastic handles back with me."

I pressed down on the uncooked bubbles with the fork.

"I stepped into the chokecherry shoots, pulled them back, and carefully cut off a few twigs. I made a bouquet out of them and carried them back with me and the tinsnips to the garage."

I picked out the middle piece and laid it on the paper-toweled plate.

"I put the tinsnips back on the shelf and carried the roses in to Noel." I turned the bacon again and pressed it.

"She was surprised. Her father used to bring her mother roses like that in the spring. She wondered where I had found them. She had seen some like them growing in the neighbor's yard.

"'There are a couple of little rosebushes growing out in the chokecherries,'" I said as she carefully took them from me and examined their yellowness and exquisite softness.

I started to pick the rest of the bacon out and lay it on the plate.

"I went back outside to do something else. After supper, while I was sitting in my chair in the living room drinking coffee, I noticed the small bouquet in a clear coffee cup full of water on top of the piano."

I turned the burner off and pushed the frying pan onto the back burner. "They stayed there until all their yellow petals fell off."

I reached for the plate and turned around. There was no one there. I went over and set the plate on the table, then went upstairs quietly to the slant-ceilinged bedroom of my youth. The bed was neatly made; it didn't look like it had been slept in. He was not there.

A note lay on the pillow. I went over, reached down, and picked it up. "I'll see you when you get there," it said.

My brow wrinkled as I read the words again. Beyond the window, in the branches of the trees, pre-dawn birds were singing up the sun. Out on the edge of town, a single hitchhiker stood and waited for a ride.

Chapter 64

Someone uses it for storage now. The pews, pulpit, organ, and baptismal font are gone. The floral carpet, which had felt the feet of generations of pastors presiding over worship and generations of Sunday School children singing "Away in a Manger" and "Jesus Loves Me" on the landing up front, remains intact. The black corduroy aisle runner that used to lie between the pews on either side is gone. The stained-glass cellophane, which had been glued onto the windows to make it look more like a church, is peeling away. The plaster is cracking.

Heaps of boards and other debris clutter the back. Broken toys are scattered on the carpet up front, along with an old white metal medicine cabinet with a faded mirror. The old store building, which the Ladner congregation purchased with the help of the Home Mission Department of the old Evangelical Lutheran Church, moved there, and converted into a church at the end of the Depression, seems so small now.

We gathered there for Uncle Martin in the wet spring of 1950, and eleven years later, we gathered for my prairie grandma. It was from there that I, no longer a child but a pastor and a man, helped bear my Uncle Arnold's casket one May.

The rock-walled basement below once held the faithful of the area: Grant and Louis Njos, the Bues, Lou Gotfredson and Lenora, the Dakes, the Graves', Oscar Moe and his sister Amanda, the Thunes, Sidney Johnson and Corrine, George Johnson, Uncle Pete, Uncle Arnold, Aunt Selma, Alfred, Lyle, and Florence, and sometimes, even Bill and Irene Stitch from Buffalo, whose place we used to live on.

They all gathered on October evenings to eat fried chicken and homemade ice cream and bid on baked goods and homespun items at the annual Ladies Aid Auction. The quilt was always saved till last, with my then-bachelor uncle, Pete, quietly holding back, attending to his pipe until it came before the auctioneer. The bidders would then turn to him, whispering one to another, while he and one or two other bidders made the quilt the most profitable item at the auction. After the bidding was over, they would go up to him. His eyes would twinkle, and he would tap his pipe, clean it out, and finger more Prince Albert into it.

"I don't know what I'm going to do with it," the most eligible bachelor in Ladner would answer as he lit his pipe back up again.

Memories seep up through the floor, tumble down off the walls. I thought I heard footsteps behind me.

But when I turned, I was alone.
It was only the wind.

Chapter 65

Time has painted the picture of prairie windmills slicing the wind with their gray metal sunflowers in my soul. Marvelous inventions.

The stem was attached to the pump plunger, and as the wind spun the flower, the pump plunger reached down and pulled water up from the subterranean depths below—for cattle and people to drink. And sometimes, in the heat of July, children stripped and swam in the wooden water tanks at the end of the cold, wet, iron pipe that stuck out from the wind-driven pumphouse pump.

They belonged to Dakota, those symbolic windmills, but they have almost disappeared from the prairie horizon. Those left miss their sunflowers, or their gray petals are twisted and useless from neglect and time. The pump plungers have been hooked up instead to electric motors, which will soon be run by coal from beneath the prairie rather than by the abundant wind above them.

So I come to Christmas in Dakota holding only a bouquet of memories— poinsettia flowers, Easter lilies, dandelions, and roses. Chaos beats against the mountains to the East and to the West, and everything in between trembles, shakes, shifts, and changes—destroying windmills, memories, and me.

But once upon a time, to lighten our darkness, to order our chaos, and to save us from our sins, once upon a time God did Christmas. And my jackrabbit heart has been caught by the coyote that howled in Bethlehem the night the angels sang. (Just think of it! God, the little Bethlehem whelp, wearin' Pampers and smackin' Similac!)

Seeds of hope are sprouting in my silent December soul, where everything else lies dormant until spring. Once upon a time, God did Christmas, and I hear the coyote of Christmas howling at me from a new day somewhere.

And I am sure that someday that little Bethlehem whelp will step out from the Right Hand of God, pick up all the broken sunflowers of Dakota, tenderly bend them back into shape, oil the mechanisms, speak his word, and like brand new things, the peaceful prairie windmills shall spin, and spin, and spin again.

Postlude

The wind was really howling as I pointed my car west towards Bowman. It pushed against my right front fender at 50 to 55 miles per hour.

Tumbleweeds, torn from their moorings, were racing across the highway, down into and through the ditches, up over the hills, and down through the draws. They came in all shapes and colors and sizes. Some were pale skeletons, while others were dark, dense, and oblong—almost flat. They rolled sideways like broken wheels through the January grass. Smaller, rounder ones bounced along and disappeared over the hills. Some hopped like jackrabbits along the horizon to the right and left. Others snagged on the barbed wire, much like some of us have been snagged on the baptismal fence.

Familiar faces began to appear in every tumbleweed, some arrayed in white, others still in mortal dress. Something within me or in the car beside me began to gather them and arrange them in a most tranquil way.

Farther down the road, an elegant mule doe stood beside the road. Her head turned slightly towards me as I approached, her wide eyes wet against the wind. I slowed. She started, leapt gracefully over the barbed wire, and glided in rhythmic bounds southeast across the stubble. It was by far the most striking thing I saw on the prairie that day.

But the sermons preached by the Spirit of Christ Jesus through the bodies of those baptized into his death are even more striking than that. They are among the most exquisite things there are in all the world. "How timely are the feet of those who bring good news."

Reeder, October 1984